My Father Is

Written by:
Jeremy Boyer

Designed by:
Stephon Beckham

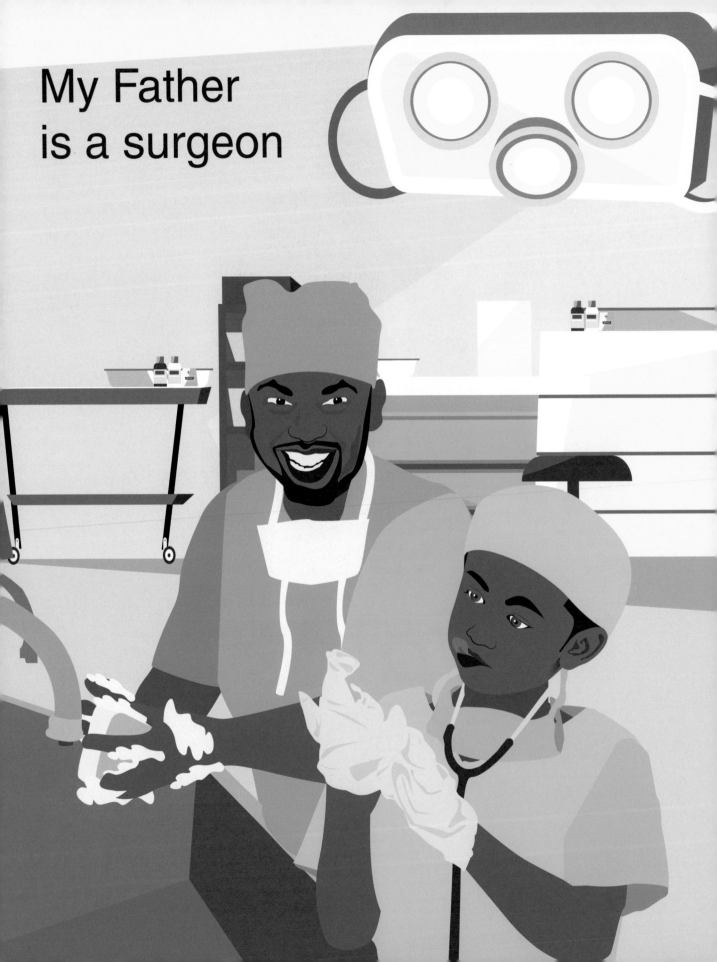

My Father
is a surgeon

My Father is
a reverend,

My Father is a chef,

My Father is,
a coach,

one time I scored a touchdown!

One time, I ate a goat...

My Father is an Author,

My Father is a great Dad, to all his sons and daughters!

My Father can
be anything,
that a Father
could want to be

Made in the USA
Columbia, SC
19 January 2024

30030828R00015